MW01194824

A quick guide to

Fight the Funk

_____

and Slay In Everyway

BY ARIE ROSE

This book was written for all of you that once had a dream as a child and somehow along the way we managed to let it slip it away. This book is a reminder that the little boy/girl that believed they could at such a young age still lives deep within. I hope this book brings him/her back out and will remind you that no matter how old you are, what your circumstances may be, you still can be everything your heart desires!

I believe in you.

 Arie R.

Table of Contents

A quick prayer before we begin

Lord,
I pray that you put your hands upon each and everyone of your children that are taking the time to read this book. I am asking you Lord that as I type these words to fill these pages that you work through me and help me fill these pages with what your children need today! Give them the strength to continue to work on themselves daily to become who they are meant to be. Provide them with clarity so that they may find their purpose on Earth!
In your name we pray!
Amen

Question

'kwesCH(ə)n/
Verb to ask questions of (someone), especially in an
official context.

1

You have a Question?
I have an answer

Why did I start with that prayer? Simple. Everything I do begins with a prayer. Prayer makes things happen. Prayer has changed me. Prayer doesn't always change the situation or the circumstances, but it will change how you view it and how you deal with it. I am nothing without the man above. This is not a book on religion, nor will I ever shove religion down your throat. However, I am here to be truthful and honest. And well, part of that is showing WHO and WHAT guides me on a daily and HOW I am able to do everything I do.

I will say it is very important and I highly recommend that if you do not believe in some greater power, you should search for something greater than you to help guide you. Whether it is a person, a goal or something else, I believe it is something we all need in our lives. I had a friend recently going through some things and she said, "Well Arie, I don't believe in God or any religion. I believe in the Universe." I replied, " Well as long as there is something you know you can turn to for guidance, something or someone that you know has your back, then that is a start." I am a firm believer that if there is no higher power in your life that you can turn to, to call on or speak to, chances are your foundation may not be sturdy when "Life" happens. It comes down to building a solid foundation, one that works with for you and with you. I don't believe you can nor should go through life alone without someone or something that you feel deep in your heart that you can count on.

My motivation, my will, my purpose stems from what I believe in and what I recieve from God. So I always give praise before I walk into any gig, job, audition, before I eat my meal, etc... This is why I can't leave such a major piece of my life out of this book. When I first began writing this book I had intended it to be an 8 page ebook and something spoke inside of me and as I began to type the pages kept flowing and growing so I told myself, "Be real, be raw and be you." So I am going to write this book exactly how I talk to my friends and maybe you may find a small mess up or a comma out of place but I didn't want anyone touching this masterpiece that stemmed from my heart. Like I said, *"Raw and real"*.

But Arie how do you know what the funk feels like?

A few years ago, I remember working day and night, night and day and not getting anywhere. I was starting to get in a major funk! I didn't want to get out of bed, I didn't want to work out. I felt physically and mentally exhausted. Have you ever been at a phase in life when you didn't want to do anything, probably weren't doing much and yet still felt tired. No energy, just super blah?

Well let me tell you, I had hit a point in my life where I was super down and I didn't know why. I looked at my life and saw so many things missing. I was STILL single, STILL a single mom, STILL struggling to keep food on the table for my child and I, STILL not where I wanted to be. How was that possible when I tried sooooo hard. My best friend invited me one day to church. I am not going to lie, I wasn't in the mood to go, but I had nothing else to do and my daughter wasn't home. She said, "Come to church with me and let's grab dinner and and drink after." Go figure, pray and then have a drink? Who does that? I said, "See you at 7:45!" I was in.

I don't know the exact words I heard that day while sitting there at Cathedral of Faith in San Jose, but this Pastor Mike guy was amazing!!! I laughed, I teared up, I was moved! At the end of the mass he said, "Someone in here today was called by God because they are feeling empty. They are tired. They need to be lifted up." He continued, " If this is you, come down to the alter so I can pray over you." I rose to my feet and walked down the alter. I remember thinking "Oh my God, that's me. He is totally talking to me." I knelt down and began to cry. I needed change. I needed something. What I didn't realize until that day was that I needed God in my life.

After that I began reading my bible and I purchased a journal where I wrote down notes from church, Ideas, dreams and letters to God. Since then my life has changed. I don't know every story in the bible, nor do I know every person in it, BUT, I do know that without it and God, I am not who I want to be.

You see this is not just about God and the bible. This is about finding what moves you. Finding what works for you. It's about letting go of what is holding you back and moving forward. We all have our secrets and pains that we carry from our past, but we cannot let those things and situations hold us down and stop us from moving into our purposeful life. Do you think we were placed here on Earth to be average? Do you think out of all the galaxies, planets etc.. that you, little ol' you.. was placed on Earth because you weren't special? This is not a coincidence.

Let me ask you another question. Do you think this book that I am writing came across your path by luck or because it's time for change? Do you believe that maybe somehow, someway deep down inside your heart you are ready for change and maybe a higher power is making things happen because you are walking into a new you?

Where does this feeling come from?

Now I don't know why we get into funks the way we do at times but I will say this, at some point something happened. Maybe you are aware of the exact moment or situation that put you in this temporary funk or maybe it just happened and you didn't even realize it was happening and poof here you are now, LOST.

There's this feeling, a certain type of emptiness that just attaches to you. You go to your job; you do your work; you see your friends, but you can't shake it off. You make plans with friends and then when it's time to get ready you find an excuse why you are not going or why you can't make it. Maybe you know that you are destined for more but feel all alone and don't even know where to start. Who do you talk to, who can help you.

Sometimes, it feels like you have to remind yourself to breathe and keep going. You feel so trapped in this moment that you can't seem to shake off. That is probably the hardest thing knowing that you don't even know where to start to get the old you back or how to begin creating the new you. Well babe let me tell you, you have two choices. You either let it take you over until you disappear, or you continue reading this and let me give you some tips on how to deal with it. I want to show you how to shake this funk off and start slaying. No matter how hard it seems you simply CANNOT let it take over! You cannot submit to the funk baby! There is this greatness inside of you, it's not gone and no you haven't lost it. We simply need to reprogram our brains and remind ourselves of who we are. We cannot let "Life" circumstances and people take away from our purpose and happiness.

I am going to share with you some things I have done in the past when I myself have fallen into my own funks as well as give you some fun to-do things at the end of every chapter to come back better than you were before. I, too, was in a funk, and just like I got out of it, rest assure you will too. Sitting here writing this book for you to read allows me to be thankful for all my funks that I have gone through in the past because without them I wouldn't have the knowledge to share with you guys nor the experience to show you how to get past this. I hope one day you can be thankful for what you are going through right now because this test is soon to be a testimony of how you did it. Now, this isn't to say that this will be your last little funk you get into, but I promise you that you will learn to laugh at future little funks when they try to kick in because you are going to be equipped with everything you need to fight them off.

one

♦♦♦♦♦♦♦♦♦♦♦♦

YOU ARE NOT
IMMUNE

So let's get started! This is day one of the journey! I hope by the time you are done reading this quick and easy read you are ready to take control back of your life. It's so easy for us to fall off a little bit but it is not okay to let ourselves remain there.

The first thing you need to do is realize, recognize and understand is that no one is immune to feeling lost from time to time. In fact, realizing that you feel lost or empty means that you are not 100% content with a certain aspect in your life. It means that you are searching to become a better you. It shows that you realize that you are capable of a deserving and amazing love. That you are deserving of a job that you really enjoy and challenges you to grow. It shows that you want to improve who you are, well, because you know there is more to you than who you are at this very moment. You are someone who is trying to improve, and that is an amazing quality.

Truth is, there are times you need to be alone. These are the difficult times that we need to take a step back and ask yourself, "What can I do differently?" I call this in my mentorship program, "The Assessment". This is when you do a hard core reality check on yourself. When you sit down and analyze where you could use some improvement in your life. We are not perfect and we should never attempt to be perfect, there is no such thing as being perfect. You should always aim to be the best version of yourself but never expect to be perfect. We are all a work in progress. My father at 71 tells me all the time that even at his age he continues to learn, to evolve and works on becoming a better man everyday. Our growing phase never ends and because of this we should never stop trying to become better.

The real problem is that a lot of us don't want to be held accountable for our faults. We don't want to admit that we are wrong, that we are not perfect. A lot of times we cheat ourselves of becoming the best versions of us because we are quick to think that it's not us, that its the outside world that is bringing us down when in reality we have the complete power to change the things that are making us unhappy at this very moment! We can not make changes that are necessary to our growth if we do not sit down, stop pointing fingers and take a look in the mirror. It's time to man up and take responsibility for our actions and accept the fact that the reason we are in our current situations are because of the habits we have and possibly the decisions we make.

It's time for us to be real with ourselves. I know I would always give people a ton of advice and tell them their hard truths when they asked what they were doing wrong, but I never gave myself my hard truths. Was I doing everything I could possible to make my life better? Was I being the very best mother I could be to my daughter so that I could be fully fulfilled in that major area in life? Was I devoting enough time to God and reading the word so that I could evolve the way I wanted to in life? I mean I had to sit down and really have a talk with myself. This, however, does not mean for you to be super hard on yourself and bring yourself down. This is simply you being an adult, taking responsibility for who you have allowed yourself to become and make changes that are necessary to blossom the very best you.

Today's task is a simple task... but you may find it takes some thought. Be real, be honest... not for me or anyone else, but for YOU.

Answer these questions honestly:

What are some of your insecurities you would like to work on:

What are some of your bad habits you need to change or cut out of your life:

Do you feel like you can be in a better position in life:

If yes, describe?

What is contributing to this funky state you are in:

What are you missing to be successful?

Do you consider yourself a motivated person? A Go-getter?

Answer these questions honestly:

Do your actions line up with what you say you want?

If you want entrepreneural freedom are you putting in the ground work to achieve that?

Do you want to make more money? Do you have a strategic plan in motion to make more?

Are you a procrastinator?

Do you find yourself making excuses for yourself on a daily or consistent basis?

Name one person in your life that you can turn to:

Good you're going to need them to keep you on track with your goals as we go through this book.

two

GRAB YOUR CHAMPAGNE

Today you are going to be your own teacher and student. I want you to do what I do any time I am feeling down. Get out a sheet of paper (and I mean seriously do this) DO NOT SKIP THIS.

I personally like to pop a bottle of champagne, pour myself a glass and put on my Pandora station to the "Los Panchos" station. You may have something else you enjoy when you need some time alone. Maybe you can run a bath and light some candles or sit on your front porch in silence. Whatever IT is that you do when you need that alone time. Now is the time to do THAT and get ready for our next step.

Draw a line down the middle and on the left of the sheet write down what is making you feel down.

THINGS MAKING YOU FEEL DOWN

- I would like to lose 10 pounds
- I would like to reduce my debt
- I need a new job that doesn't demand 60 hours a week from me
- I am not spending much time with my family
- ....
- ....

Everyone's list will be different but include all the things that you know for sure are making you feel this way. It can be your recent weight gain, maybe it is the relationship you are in. It can very well be your job or the way you act when you are angry. I know some people may feel like you can be a better partner or a better parent. Whatever area you feel you can improve in and you simply aren't currently happy with write it down.

Once you are done with that list (the right hand side is still empty, we will get to it in a second) I want you to go through that list and get two color highlighters, let's say yellow and pink. With the yellow highlighter I want you to highlight anything on that list that is in your control. These are action items that we can set goals and change. With the pink highlighter, highlight things that are out of your control.

For example if you are unhappy because you are currently the heaviest you have been then highlight that yellow because we can definitely change that on our own. If you are down because you were laid off highlight that pink. Things that are in the past are out of our control. Just like the way someone treats us is out of our control, however we have the control whether or not we continue to put up with it. Once you are done you are going to write on the right hand side what you can do to change the yellow. Every yellow has a solution, it may not seem like an easy one but somehow, someway it can be fixed.

THINGS MAKING YOU FEEL DOWN	SOLUTION
• I would like to lose 10 pounds	Start a new diet
• I would like to reduce my debt	Cut my credit cards up
• My boss is not fair	N/A
• I need a new job that doesn't demand 60 hours a week from me	Fix my resume and start job hunting
• I am not spending much time with my family	Make dinner for my family every Tuesday

M Y
D E C L A R A T I O N

I, _____, on this day, the ___ of _____, promise to let go of any dead weight that is holding me back from becoming the person I was put on Earth to become. I promise to release, forgive and move on from anything that has held me a prisoner to my past. I know I am fully capable and equipped with every tool and talent needed to achieve everything my heart desires. I am ready to receive all my blessings and do whatever it takes to live a purpose filled life.

This is my declaration!

_____
CEO of my life

three

DREAM BIG

Now that we have this amazing list highlighted in yellow we simply cannot let it go to waste! It's time to work on your goals baby! Some of you may have some very big goals on your list and that is great, after all it's our duty to dream big. Did you forget we serve an amazing God, a God that wants to bless you in abundance. If we do not dream big and pray big then we will forever stay mediocre. Our blessings are only as big as we make them.

I went to speak at Dash Radio in Hollywood on "The Fix" last month ago and they asked me what I meant when I said, "You have to stretch your mind in order to receive all your blessings that God has in store for you." My reply went something like this.

"Imagine that I come to your house with a bag full of money. Let's say I have a million dollars cash in a duffle bag and I tell you to grab a bag so I can give all this money to you. You take a moment to look around and grab a shoe box where you keep your current money in and tell me, 'This is the only room I have left.' So you are telling me that because you do not have more "room" you are going to let me walk back out of here with my million dollars that I wanted to give to you?"

This is the same thing we do with our thinking. We shut down the endless possibilities, the abundance of blessings with our names on it because we don't think we are deserving enough or are equipped enough to handle it. We don't believe we have the capacity for our blessings. We sell ourselves short. ***WE SAY NO TO OUR BLESSINGS BEFORE THEY EVEN ARRIVE TO OUR FRONT DOOR.***

As impossible as our goals may seem remember we serve a very possible God. This is not the time to get anxiety over your list or to start to question if you have what it takes to accomplish your goals. I am here to tell you that you are fully equipped and capable of accomplishing any task at hand to crush your goals.

I owned 2 successful hair salons for 7 years with my sister and mother, yes I am a licensed cosmetologist. No matter how busy I was with hair and all the amazing clients I had, I was never fully satisfied. I would always get phone calls from people in the industry asking me to be a video host, model or interview red carpet events. I knew that was my calling because anytime the camera's and lights turned on, I came to life. I began calling friends from local stations and asking if they were hiring or needed an intern. Everyone said the same thing, "Sorry Arie, but you don't have any experience to be hired and we can't allow you to intern unless you are enrolled in school." So guess what I did? I called my mom feeling defeated yet determined and I said, "Mom, I am not happy. I do not see myself doing hair in 40 years, I want to close the salons down and go back to school if you and my sister agree." I held my breath and thought "What in the world are you doing?" You see just like anyone else I had self doubt. I had everything salon owners and stylist dream of, was I being selfish? My mom replied, "Ok, I support you 100% and so does your sister so let's sell the salons."

Eight months later I walked on campus as San Jose State University to begin working on my B.A. in TV/Film/Radio Production, 3 months after that I began my first internship with Estrella TV in San Francisco, 6 months after that I interned at Mundo FOX in their production department. One month into that internship I created my very own segment that went live on television in the Bay Area 3 times a week, I was also a co-host on air for that segment. Two years after that I graduated with my degree from San Jose State and exactly 6 months after I crossed the stage I signed my very first contract for my own show that I created with a major company in New York.

Sometimes it may be hard to think of the dreams you had for your life before you lost yourself in the chaos of life? In a perfect world with nothing to hold you back what would you love to be, have, or do? What is it that your soul is aching for? Whatever it is, let it come back to you. It's never to late to switch it up. Those dreams and goals are still there waiting for you to come for them.

Dream baby

If money, time or anything else was an issue, what would you be doing today?

What are some things you can do to help make this possible ?

Deep deep down inside what makes you genuinely happy?

Why are you not doing more of that?

What are you willing to do to make these changes?

Time to Slay a Goal

You can do this for each item highlighted in pink but this
week we are going to focus on one action item that we are
going to tackle

This weeks goal:

Breakdown your goal into steps 5 steps needed to tackle
it this week.

Day 1:

Day 2:

Day 3:

Day 4:

Day 5:

Time to Slay a Goal

What can you do today (not tomorrow) to begin working towards this goal?

What distraction will you cut out to make sure you stay focused on this goal?

TO DO:

- Write every step on a post it note & check it off once you accomplish it
- Remember that one person you could count on? Call them, tell them about it and ask them to stay on you about it
- Set daily reminders in your phone
- Once you accomplish this goal *CELEBRATE*!

four

WHAT FEARS

Stop giving power to your fears! Stop being so scared of failing. Most of us are afraid of failing so bad that we do not even begin to try. The crazy thing we fail to realize is that if we give up before we even try, then we have already failed!

We give so much life to our fears that we forget our true hearts desires, therefor, we allow our happiness to swipe away from under our feet without even knowing. We would rather not go for it and be miserable than to simply try! Do you know how many things I have done that scare me straight shitless?

How is this for a reminder, did you know that we are born with zero fears? As we go through life we allow society to mold us, manipulate our minds and we begin to create our own fears. When we are born we are innocent, our minds are not contaminated by peoples opinions or by what we see or learn from society. Our fears are self made, we create these fears inside our minds and then allow them to have control over us.

I am not going to lie and act like I'm tough and have zero fears because just like you I am human and yes I have some fears, however I have learned to analyze and be real with myself when I know that I am not progressing with something in life because I am allowing my fears to hold me back. This is when I sit and have the "What is the worst thing that can happen Arie" talk with myself. I sit down and put things in perspective and proceed with that I know has to be done regardless of how scary it may seem at the time. Have you ever done something that you were so scared of and after you did it you almost laughed at yourself and thought " Why the heck was I so damn scared to do that in the first place?"

I'm going to give you the perfect silly girly example right now. I don't know how many of you get waxed but this is a true confession of a fear of mine. I get my lip waxed and if you ladies get it done too you know that shit hurts! So everytime I lay down to get my eyebrows and lips waxed I am already building my nerves up thinking about how painful this is about to be. Then when my girl Nancy starts to put the baby powder at the top of my lip and I smell the scent I swear my hands start to get sweaty. Mind you I have done this a million times. Fast forward, as she is about to pull the darn wax strip off, I squeeze my eyes so tight because I know this is about to hurt and RIPPPP, she's done and I'm laughing now because of how silly I just looked. Needless to say, 6 weeks later I'm back with Nancy to do it all over again. Moral of the story our fears are as big as we create them to be.

It's time to stop living in a sheltered box and start tackling these fears one at time. You want to make a fun to do list? How about this, write down all your fears and tackle them off that list. How's that for a start.

This stage you are going through is what I call the growing stage and it doesn't happen by staying in your comfort box where everything is familiar. Challenge yourself to do something that scares you. Go on that trip alone, call that guy and ask him on a date, go and ask your boss for that raise! That is what I like to call stepping out of your comfort zone. It's this place where you stretch yourself enough to continue to grow and evolve into who you are meant to be. So babe, what's the first thing that came to mind for you to do? Go and do that!

What are some of your fears?

Even the toughest strongest people on Earth have hidden fears. Dig deep and write them down here. How can you overcome these? Are you scared of flying, driving, changes? Are you afraid of what people may think or of failing? Write them all down and figure out how to conquer them!

Self Made Fear #1

How can I overcome it?

Self Made Fear #2

How can I overcome it?

Self Made Fear #3

How can I overcome it?

five

REMEMBER WHO THE FXCK YOU ARE

Don't forget who the f*ck you are! It's so easy for us to feel like mush sometimes. I think this is such a major aspect when it comes to being in a funk. I feel like I talk about this every time I speak in front of an audience or on a panel. We live in such a public era. Nothing is sacred, everything is exposed. So what happens when everything is public, well we end up looking at everyone's lives comparing them to ours. We begin to become envious of what others have, even though I believe a lot of what we see isn't the way it really seems. We can get so caught up that we fail to acknowledge our own blessings, our own talents and sometimes even our own worth.

If this has happened to you, you are not alone.

I remember I had a friend of mine a few years ago who asked me to help her break in to the scene. Super sweet young girl who barely knew many people. I would give her advice and tell her when certain places were looking for models or what not. Well unlike me she faced her fears and moved to LA and left her family and friends behind to chase her dream. I noticed that almost instantly her followers grew, she was getting roles in films and commercials, getting sponsorships etc.. Well I found myself inspecting everything she did which at first seemed to me like I was just trying to see what was working for her so I could try and do the same thing. I mean I was excited for her and I wanted to get some tips so I could duplicate what she was doing.

What I thought was the smart approach turned out not to be for a few reasons:

I realized I became envious of what she had and I began forgetting about what I had. I was losing who I genuinely was because I was trying to be like someone else and forgetting that I had my own lane and my own talents. I began losing focus on my purpose because I was too busy looking at the next girl's purpose and winnings. I was so focused on someone else's garden that I was not tending to my own plot. I wasn't winning because I wasn't working on my purpose, period. I was praying all the way wrong at this time. I would ask God, "Why can't I have those opportunities?"

You may think this is a bit much but when we don't focus on what God has given us we lose! Point blank period. We forget who we are, what we stand for and who we are destined to become.

I am so thankful now that God cleared up my eyes. I began praying so differently. It was a true moment of growth for me. I believe that this was my "Wake up and fight the funk" moment. This is the moment that I, Arie Rose, began walking into my season of purpose and an overhaul of blessings.

I began praying like this:

'Lord, I know you are there. I know you are watching over me. I know that you feel what I am going through and you know this is not me. I don't know where I lost myself, but Lord help me find myself again. Clear my eyes so that I can focus on you and my path. Speak to my heart so that I may find MY purpose. Give me the strength to continue on my journey to become who you want me to become and most importantly protect me from any distractions that the enemy sends my way when I am focused on my journey. AMEN."

The growth. Oh My God, My growth. I am still amazed at how much prayer has changed me. I still smile and thank God everyday for changing me and helping me evolve into the woman I am. You see I had forgotten who the F*ck I was. And let me tell you, once I remembered who I was and I got her back.. boy was it on!

*Lesson: Remember who the f*ck YOU are*

Remember who you are

What are your favorite things about yourself?

What are you really good at?

What do people compliment you on most:

People love you because _____.

Write down a proud moment:

Now, remember these on a daily and when you begin to feel down remember how amazing you truly are!

REPROGRAM
YOUR THOUGHTS

I don't think enough people on Earth realize how powerful our thoughts are. Our thoughts are what we make of our lives. When we set our thoughts into motion with our intentions, the universe responds through the law of attraction. Have you ever taken the time to read about the Law of Attraction? Did you know that every thought is like an electrical impulse, we are like a radio station that transmits our thoughts by sending out a certain frequency. The frequencies of our thoughts are vibrations. The vibrations of our thoughts attract like a magnet to other thoughts on the same frequency. This means that whatever we send out is what comes back to us like a boomerang.

Have you ever heard people say, "You have the power to change your circumstance?" This is because any change in our lives begins within us. It begins with how we think. The life you are living now is not permanent. If we don't like what we are attracting or the way things are going for us we have the power to change how we are experiencing life by changing the thoughts we are creating in our minds. Our frequency then changes, as does everything we attract. If we continue to think the same every day, how can we expect to change our lives. If you are always negative how can you expect to attract anything positive in your life.

Think of a time where you encountered a negative person. Think of that one co-worker that always complains or is always in a bad mood. Does that person attract you to them? If they were to invite you to lunch you may actually think to yourself, "Is this a lunch I am going to enjoy?" This is not to be taken in the context that we should be mean or decline people who need love, however, it's an example of how this attraction thing works.

When you begin to think positive thoughts positive things come into your life. Opportunities begin to flow towards you, doors begin to open that you never imagined before. This is because what our minds think we believe. Our thoughts go far beyond more than creating our destiny, it overflows into what we deem possible to do in our lives. Our thoughts affect our every move literally. If we think we can't then chances are we won't be able to do it. How many times have you encountered a situation where you questioned your own ability to get it done and almost failed before you even tried.

I went for a hike the other day with some good friends of mine and I was going up this pretty steep hill that I could've sworn was going to kill me. About 40 min non stop uphill I felt my calf start to cramp up. One of my friends said, "Come on, let's just get to the top, you are almost there. There is about 10 minutes at the most to finish." About 2 minutes up I looked at her and said, "You guys are on your own." At that moment I had accepted defeat, I was ready and more than willing to give up.

She began laughing, kept walking and shouted back down at me, "That's why you workout with people so they can motivate you. You can do this." I laughed but surely did not continue up. I figured I would rather walk down alone than die getting to the top, even if it was only 10 more minutes to the top.

As I stood there catching my breath three ladies came walking up the hill. Two of the ladies were ahead and one fell a little behind. She had a walking stick and was breathing hard drenched in sweat. One of the ladies as she passed me up yelled back at her, "Come on Anne repeat your affirmations like I showed you. I watched at the lady in the back wipe her sweat, stand tall and began saying outloud, "I am strong, I am young, I have what it takes in me to climb up this hill."

I looked at her and said, "Thank you Anne." She said, "I'm sorry?" She had no idea what she had just done for me. I replied, "You just motivated me to motivate myself."

See the thing is that if we do not believe that we can then we will never be able to. Even if we have some amazing friends by our side on the way to the top that encourage us and speak to our inner warrior, if we do not believe we can, we won't. As Anne pushed herself uphill I walked along with her and we recited these affirmations together. I gave myself the power and the strength I needed to get up that hill, to push a little more and to dig a little deeper. Now I am not going to lie, by the time I reached the top I really thought I was going to die, but I went back down the hill so happy that I pushed myself and went the extra mile.

I believe that if you say something is hard it will be hard to do. Things are only as hard as we make them. Self talk can make you or break you! Do you remember being in high school and taking algebra? I remember being so frustrated that I didn't understand all these numbers and letters jumbled up together. I mean after all why mix numbers and letters. HA. I remember how much I use to tell myself how hard it was and now looking back it was only harder because I made my mind think that. What about when you are on the treadmill and you keep looking at the time, boy does it go slow and endless because you are telling yourself every second how much more you have got to go and it feels like an eternity, so difficult to finish. However, if you throw the towel over the machine so you don't see the time and put on your favorite album or catch your favorite netflix show on your phone, boy do those minutes fly by. What do you mean I have been on here for 30 minutes already?

This was such an important lesson and reminder that anytime I feel like maybe I can't do something all I have to do is tell myself that I can and I will.

Action thoughts

What is something you are currently struggling to accomplish?

Why do you feel you are having a hard time accomplishing it?

Do your thoughts have anything to do with you not being able to accomplish the task at hand?

Tell yourself over and over everyday that you have what it takes to get it done baby! Speak it till you believe it!

seven

◆◆◆◆◆◆◆◆◆◆◆

Don't take it personal babe

This is probably the hardest thing I have ever had to learn. I am a very passionate person when it comes to anything I do in life, anything I believe in and anybody I love. So when things don't go according to how I have them planned out in my mind, I find myself frustrated and over emotional because I was so passionate about the vision I had and the outcome I expected. However, those are just that, my "outcomes I expected". I have finally come to realize after being let down a million times by my own expectations that I simply cannot set my expectations on other people. I shouldn't expect others to do what I would do in certain situations because every single mind is a world of its own.

I have had bosses I have worked for that I bent over backwards for and I never received a simple "Thank you." We cannot expect for people to do for us what we do for them. It is our very own expectations on certain situations that will be our very own downfall. If you do not control your emotions and realize that your emotions are the only things you can control, you could very well take it personal and end up saying/doing something you shouldn't or that you may regret down the road. You need to realize that not everyone is like you, not everyone will do what you would do in certain situations and that you simply cannot expect for others to be and think like you.

When you take things personal you allow yourself to be vulnerable, however, we can completely control how personal we take things. Although it may seem like it's always about us, most of the time it's simply not. How people treat you has nothing to do with you and and everything to do with them. It speaks volumes on their character and shows you who they really are. Don't allow anyone from the outside to have a hold on your emotions personally or in business.

When you are in a situation where another party is involved try not to set any expectations on them. Expectations can lead to disappointments. If you are reading this and nodding your head then chances are that you too, just like myself, have let ourselves down by setting our own expectations on others. This is not to say that you should accept any less that what you believe you deserve in your heart but merely to analyze the situation and if you feel like you will not get out of it what you put into it then you should rethink if you should be investing your time in that situation.

Sometimes I find that I tend to over give on everything I do in life. I am a natural giver by heart. So there are a lot of times where what I give out is not reciprocated. Again, you cannot nor should you expect everyone to give you what you give in return. This is in all aspects in life. When it comes to family, relationships and in your career. I have trained my mind to think for the best and simply not set expectations. The only thing I put expectations on are my emotions, what I do and my prayers! I know that I am only in control of myself and that at the end of the day regardless of things going my way or not, God is in control of my life. He knows what he is doing with my life, what my journey looks like and what the big picture is. Don't overthink things or go crazy observing what others do or don't do. They are not our problem, what we do is the only thing that should make a difference in our lives.

Something to think about when you feel yourself beginning to take something personal is to ask yourself will you care in a year? Chances are most things you will say no to which will make it easier to move past it and focus on things that matter.

The hard truth about my expectations

Did you nod at some point with what you just read? If so, what are certain situations that you have set expectations on others and in the end let yourself down or took it personal?

What can you do next time a situation arises so that you can avoid setting expectations on certain people and situations?

Are you currently going through a let down? If so, what is the cause of this let down. Did you set expectations on something and now you feel let down?

If you said yes to the last question, let it go babe. Learn from it and stop putting expectations on others. Don't take it personal, after all, we have no control over others actions.

eight

SLAY HABITS

It is important to build **GREAT** habits. I emphasize *great habits* because most of us have created so many habits in our lives that do us no good. We watch certain TV shows and listen to certain things that we do not realize how much impact they have on our lives. We don't even question whether these things we are letting into our brain have negative impact in our lives. We do not step back to see if the habits things and people create in our lives are good for us or not. Have you ever sat back and analyzed the people who you allow to be around you and take up your time on a daily or even on the weekends?

Not too long ago my father showed me a video he came across about John D. Rockefeller Sr. If you don't know who John D. Rockefeller Sr. was well according to Wikipedia John "was an American oil industry business magnate and philanthropist. He is widely considered the wealthiest American of all time, and the richest person in modern history." Mr. Rockefeller was born into a modest circumstance home in upstate New York. Long story short, according to this video that I watched, Mr. Rockefeller had come across these men in New York one morning while he was a young boy and they were talking about a business meeting that they held everyday at the local coffee shop. He had asked the men if he could come to the meeting to simply listen and the men had laughed at him. John began to save money from the money he earned everyday and would go to the coffee shop, buy a coffee and sit at the next table to listen, watch and observe these business men. The coffee shop owners thought he was a weird little boy but they couldn't kick him out because he was a paying customer. Who knew back then that this was the beginning of America's wealthiest man of all time.

I share this story because it had such a major impact on my life. I sat back and had a major reality check. Who was I learning my habits from? Who was I letting impact my life on a daily basis? Were the people I was hanging out with all the time creating habits for me that would make me better in life? Could I become successful with the circle of friends I hung out with? Have you ever wondered if maybe you just weren't surrounding yourself with the right people and cultivating great habits?

> "Motivation is what gets you started ,
> Habit is what keeps you going"
> -Jim Rohn

So what are some great habits that we should create? Well let's go over some of them. These are not in order by preference nor are they the only ones, however, I am putting the ones that have been the most effective for me.

Get that booty up early baby!

Get up an hour earlier. People always complain that they only have 24 hours in a day and although that may be true, the real truth is you may just be sleeping them away.

> *"Early to bed and early to rise makes*
> *a man healthy, wealthy and wise."*
> *-Benjamin Franklin*

Visualize & Manifest

Early hours can bring about some amazing reflections. Enjoy the quiet and take some time to map out your day before the craziness begins. Think about your goals and what you need to get done for the day. When you take the time to visualize your goals you are putting them out to the Universe to manifest! Take whatever notes you need to make sure your day will productive!

> *"When you visualize, then*
> *you materialize."*
> *-Denis Waitley*

Get going!

Morning workouts not only give you a boost of energy, they pump you up, ensuring your senses are up and running. You'll feel ready to tackle any problem that comes your way. I like to set my alarm 30-60 minutes earlier than I need to be up to get in my morning workout. I know that if I wait till later I will get caught up with work, my daughter or something else that will lead me to not getting any workout time in. My workouts in the A.M. are my top priority because they allow me to start my day feeling amazing!

> *"Wake up and Slay the Day!"*
> *-Arie Rose*

Forget the TV & pick up a book!

Reading increases your imagination, creativity, vocabulary, memory and decreases stress. Not to mention reading makes your smarter. Pick up a book on a new hobby of interest, a cook book or even a fun romance novel to take you away from the daily stress.

> *"Reading is the key feature in every single*
> *successful person I have ever met."*
> *-Mario Batali*

Meditate:
Oprah, Rupert Murdoch, Russell Simmons and tons more have all attributed mediation as a huge piece of their success. Some of you as soon as you see the word are thinking "Arie I don't know how to do that." Well shout out to Youtube and Google for having videos and articles on anything you want to learn to do. There isn't one technique for this, so research and try. See what works for you!

> *"To the mind that is still, the whole universe*
> *surrenders."*
> *- Lao Tzu*

Say no!

Successful people realize that by saying "no" to negativity, extra work and activities that waste time, they can focus on what is crucial to their success. You can't say "yes" to everyone putting yourself last and expect to succeed or become better. Learn to say "no" to others from time to time and say "yes" to more of what you need and feels right for you. If you continue to say "yes" to everyone or everything that comes your way, you may find yourself too distracted and not accomplishing things that will benefit your future.

> *"The difference between successful people and very successful people is that successful people say no to almost everything."*
> *-Warren Buffett*

Be still & Be patient:

Waking up early offers you opportunities that few get to enjoy – watch the sun rise, hear the sound of birds chirping, and just be still. We are always on the move. Sit and enjoy the morning calm. It's a brief time where you can be alone with your thoughts. Just breathe.

> *"Everything comes to you at the right time. Be patient and trust the process"*
> *-Unknown*

Choose up!

Be selective with the people you choose to spend your time with. If you are not improving and advancing in your life with your circle then maybe you are sitting at the wrong table. It's okay to meet new people and make friends with like minded dreams and ambition. This is your life! Choose up!

> *If you hang around 5 confident people, you'll be the 6th.*
> *If you hang around 5 intelligent people, you'll be the 6th.*
> *If you hang around 5 millionaires, you'll be the 6th.*
> *If you hang around 5 idiots, you'll be the 6th.*
> *If you hang around 5 broke people, you'll be the 6th.*
> *-Unknown*

Create new habits

Which habits that you just read stood out to you the most?

What habits that you just read about do you possess currently?

What habits from this chapter will you apply to your day?

What changes do you need to make to enable some of these new habits in your life?

Create new habits

Pick one habit today to enforce in your life immediately.

In order to accomplish this here are some tips:

- Set your mind to enforcing this habit in your life for 30 days.
- Set a daily reminder to do this
- Set a weekly reward in your phone calendar for sticking to it.

Remember, it is important to keep each habit reasonable, so that you can maintain momentum and make the behavior as easy as possible to accomplish. If you are setting a new habit that takes more time out of your day try splitting it into 2 segments.

*"Obsessed is the word the lazy
use to describe the dedicated
-Unknown*

nine

TALK < ACTION

Do more than you speak of. Action is what makes you who you really are. Your actions, your hustle is what is going to take you to the next level in life. You can sit in bed all day with ideas, plans and dreams but if you don't get up and get to it you will wake up tomorrow and the day after and the day after that in the same spot you are in today.

Don't be a person with short arms reaching for the stars. Be the person that when you speak of doing something, people know that it is going to get done. Your word is the only thing you have. You only have one name, what type of reputation is attached to it. Are you the type of person that people say "If she says she will do it please believe it will get done" or are you the type of person that people say "She says she will start her diet today but she always says that and doesn't". If you are one of the people that is all talk and no action then its time to make some drastic changes in this area. You can't get farther in life sending out empty promises into the world. People like helping people who are "movers and shakers", the people that get things done on a daily. These are the people that have opportunities raining on them because they have built a solid reputation based on their work ethic.

There is nothing worse than a person that has a million excuses as to why they didn't get something done. I feel like when something needs to get done and it doesn't get done we have a "valid" excuse as to why it didn't get done or why we can't get it done.

I have another friend of mine that moved to Los Angeles to chase her dream. She had been there for 2 months and had not worked yet. We went to dinner one day and I introduced her to a friend that we bumped into. I told them to stay connected because they were both in the same industry and I overheard her tell my friend that she was excited to connect with her because she didn't have any friends in the LA area yet. She had not met anyone since she had moved to LA. My immediate reaction was "what the f*ck". So here is something you need to know about me, if I love and care about you I am going to dish it to you raw and tell you exactly what you probably don't want to hear. I have never been a yes friend. I am that friend that starts with, "Listen, don't get mad or offended, but I'm about to tell you something about yourself." It's never easy being told about where you are messing up but everyone needs a friend that is going to tell you and set you straight.

Back to the story. So as soon as my friend was gone and we were back to just the two of us I looked at her and I said, "Amiga, why don't you have any friends in LA yet, or even acquaintances?" She replied, "Oh, well because I don't know anyone here to hang out with and I haven't gone out." I was in complete shock. I said, "You mean to tell me that you left your entire family behind, your friends and the city you grew up in to come to Los Angeles to pursue your career and you have yet to make one connection AND you've been here for almost 2 months?" She said, " Well I haven't gotten any gigs while I have been here so I don't have any other way to meet friends or people." Oh my Jesus, I almost stopped breathing and passed out on the spot. Yes I am a little over dramatic, ha, but that is how I felt. I replied, "Listen, the fact that you haven't even gotten a gig in 2 months or some type of work is crazy. There are Facebook groups to connect with people in your area, you can use hashtags that related to your line of work in your area and you can see where they go, heck you can slide in their dm's and ask them personally." The truth is people are always happy to help, if they are not then they probably are not the right people that you need to help you.

Listen the moral of this story is to stop making excuses. Excuses create average people. Excuses are the biggest dream killers and the reason why most people don't ever accomplish their goals. Stop making excuses and making it okay to be where you are at right now. If you are not happy then do something to change your situation. No one has a perfect life or a perfect situation so just deal with your reality. If your reality is your obstacle, the thing standing between you and your dreams then figure out a way to go around it, to work around it. There is always a loop hole to help you get things done. There is always someone that is willing to lend a helping hand. If you are reading this and thinking, "No Arie, I have no one willing to help me." Guess what, you don't have anyone willing to help you because you have set that in your mind so deep that you have stopped looking for people. You have accepted that excuse and accepted the defeat. If I am hungry and I only have 25 cents to my name and I need a dollar to eat, please believe I am going to flip the entire house upside down until I find 75 more cents to get me what I need. When you are hungry you will figure it out. When are you going to stop making excuses and allow yourself to continue to be defeated by "life". Do you know that what you are going through may not be because of "life" but maybe it's your "life choices". Do you know that your current situation isn't your final destination? Do you know that if you try a little harder, go the extra mile, you can change your current situation?

Are you ready to stop vacationing and get to work?

Reality Check

There is a goal I want to achieve but I am making excuses to get it done.

My Reality is I don't have what it takes to get it done

I simply don't have enough hours in a day

If I had more money I could get it done

If I had a friend or someone to help me I would totally do it

*If you said yes to any of these listed above, cut it out. Stop making excuses! Get it done!

What excuses are you getting rid of today?

1)

2)

3)

ten

◆◆◆◆◆◆◆◆◆◆◆
TIME TO SLAY THE OLD YOU AWAY

This is it, the time is now. No more old you. You have everything you need to tackle every single dream your heart is screaming at you for. There is no room in your life for anymore excuses. We don't know if tomorrow is promised or what our circumstances may be when we wake up tomorrow. So the time is now to take full advantage and make our lives the very best we can. It is time to start reaching for the stars with every single inch of our bodies. Whatever reason we have given ourselves as to why it is ok to keep on living the way we are has expired. That reason is no longer valid. There is no reason why we aren't improving and increasing in all areas in our lives. It's time we begin to stop focusing on what we don't have and start focusing on what we are working for. If you want it bad enough you will have it. It's time to strive for what you really want and to make sure it is what you really want. There is no time for second guesses or to sit around and wait for things to magically happen while you walk around every day unhappy and unfulfilled. It is time to deal with your reality and realize that no one's reality is perfect but we can chose to work around it and get things done. So you have a full time job, 2 kids and a husband.. That is so amazing, figure out how your husband can help you so you have an hour or two to work on your dreams. Oh, you are tired by the time the kids lay down for you to begin working at that time on your dreams, well maybe you should consider waking up earlier before everyone to get the quiet time you need. Set your coffee to automatically brew at 5 am if that is the only time you have to work on you. Put the effort in, you have to really want it and go for it full heartedly.

This morning I had breakfast with a close friend of mine and he was laughing telling me a story about his son.

His son has a busy day every day because of his school and sporting activities after school. So last night his son has basketball practice an hour away and they didn't get home till almost 10pm, his bedtime is usually 9 pm. He was super upset at the end of the night because he had to go straight to bed and wasn't able to play any video games yesterday. So my friend told him, "Son, if you don't have enough time in a day to do things you want to do then you should consider waking up earlier to get more things done in your day." His son complained because he wakes up as it is at 6:45 am for school. Well the next day my friend went to his sons room to wake him up and his son was awake already playing his video games. My friend said he couldn't help but giggle.

If there is something that you really want and need to get done then you are going to do whatever it takes to make it happen. You always hear people say, "We all have the same 24 hours in a day, it's what you do with them that makes a difference." I must say that is one of the truest statements ever made. It's up to you what you decide to do with your 24 hours. Are you going to sleep in or are you going to wake up with some good positive energy and hustle? Are you going to keep making excuses as to why you can't do it or are you going to start telling yourself all the reasons why it's easy for you to get it done? Will you sign up for that night class you have been contemplating to get that degree you have been wanting for years or say it's too late?

Why is it that we talk ourselves out of amazing things that are meant for us in our lives. Why do we treat ourselves that way and make ourselves believe that we are undeserving?

It's time to accept that you have been bullshitting yourself and start working for what you really want. You deserve to rise to your full potential and you deserve all the blessings with your name on them that are waiting for you to rise up and receive them. We serve an amazing God and he wants you to have an amazing life. A life full of love, blessings and opportunities. The only way you are going to get that is to snap out of it, stop making excuses and dedicate yourself to your success.

Remember, it is not too late to get on it. A college degree attained at 70 is still a college degree. A million dollars attained at 50 is still a million dollars. A Mercedes purchased at 40 is still a Mercedes. Don't let anyone's success timeline fool you into thinking it is too late. No matter what age you are it is never too late to follow your dreams.

So what are you waiting for... it's time to SLAY!

66

Be the
HUSTLE
&
Slay baby

Arie Rose

#SlayInEveryway

10 Affirmations

to repeat & remember daily

I am perfect the way I am

I am worthy of all the blessings God has in store for me

I am ready to become the best version of "ME" possible

I am fully equipped with every tool needed to succeed

Every storm has an end

Every experience I have is perfect for my growth

I forgive myself & set myself free

I am not alone

Every decision I make is the right one for my path

Everything I walk towards fills my life with prosperity

Acknowledgments

Special thanks to Michelle Picar aka my Manang Mimi for checking in on me often and making sure I kept writing my book. It's the littlest things that make the biggest impacts on peoples lives. She was the first one who said she wanted a signed copy before I even thought of printing this book. Most of you may not know but this book was created with the intent to build my email list and it was originally suppose to be an 8 page E-book. Low and behold my fingers kept moving and here we are far past 8 pages. So Michelle, thank you for always believing in me and most importantly never laughing at my crazy wild and huge dreams of mine. I love you! Thanks to Carl The Young Executive for holding my hand (virtually) every step of the way with this book. From beginning to end you showed me the way! Thanks to my friend Dave Diggs for showing me that it was possible to do this, for showing me how to start. You are the reason why I felt that I could right this book to begin with. Thank you for inspiring me even when you didn't know you were.
&
To everyone who read my first book, THANK YOU!

Xoxo,
Arie Rose

Slay in Everyway

Slaying isn't just about looks or your clothes, slaying is about being confident from the inside, it's about knowing how to show up and show out. It's about being a well rounded person and finding the true meaning of happiness. It's about finding your purpose and killen the game to your full capacity.

Follow @SlayInEveryway
Use hashtag #SlayInEveryway

More info www.iamarierose.com

About Arie Rose

I am a strong Latina, a mother & a lover of life... I am also a producer, TV Host, Motivational speaker, mentor and author. I am in pursuit of my dreams. The only thing I fear is never accomplishing my dreams and goals. Apparently, if you never quit you'll get there someday.

-A

Make sure to follow
@iamarierose on all social media
www.iamarierose.com

Made in the USA
Middletown, DE
09 June 2018